KU-244-375

LIFE CYCLE OF AN...

Apple

Revised and Updated

Angela Royston

Heinemann

LIBRARY

www.heinemannlibrary.co.uk

Visit our website to find out more information about Heinemann Library books.

To order:

☏ Phone +44 (0) 1865 888066

▤ Fax +44 (0) 1865 314091

▣ Visit www.heinemannlibrary.co.uk

Heinemann Library is an imprint of Capstone Global Library Limited, a company incorporated in England and Wales having its registered office at 7 Pilgrim Street, London, EC4V 6LB - Registered company number: 6695582

"Heinemann" is a registered trademark of Pearson Education Limited, under licence to Capstone Global Library Limited

Text © Capstone Global Library Limited 1998, 2009
Second edition first published in hardback and paperback in 2009
The moral rights of the proprietor have been asserted.

All rights reserved. No part of this publication may be reproduced in any form or by any means (including photocopying or storing it in any medium by electronic means and whether or not transiently or incidentally to some other use of this publication) without the written permission of the copyright owner, except in accordance with the provisions of the Copyright, Designs and Patents Act 1988 or under the terms of a licence issued by the Copyright Licensing Agency, Saffron House, 6–10 Kirby Street, London EC1N 8TS (www.cla.co.uk). Applications for the copyright owner's written permission should be addressed to the publisher.

Edited by Adrian Vigliano, Harriet Milles, Diyan Leake
Designed by Kimberly R. Miracle and Tony Miracle
Original illustrations © Capstone Global Library Limited 1998, 2009
Illustrated by Alan Fraser
Picture research by Tracy Cummins
Originated by Chroma Graphics (Overseas) Pte Ltd
Printed in China by South China Printing Company Ltd

ISBN 978 0 431 99946 3 (hardback)
13 12 11 10 09
10 9 8 7 6 5 4 3 2 1

ISBN 978 0 431 99964 7 (paperback)
13 12 11 10 09
10 9 8 7 6 5 4 3 2 1

British Library Cataloguing in Publication Data
Royston, Angela.
  Life cycle of an apple. -- 2nd ed.
  1. Apples--Life cycles--Juvenile literature.
  I. Title II. Apple
  571.8'2373-dc22

Acknowledgements
We would like to thank the following for permission to reproduce photographs: Age Fotostock pp. 24 (© Sarah Cuttle), 27 (© Dave Rusk); Holt Studios International pp. 5 (© Inga Spense), 6 (© Nigel Cattlin), 13 (© Nigel Cattlin); © Jupiter Images p. 26; NHPA photoshot p. 29 top left (© Stephen Dalton); Photolibrary pp. 20 (© Oxford Scientific Library/ Carson Baldwin Jr.), 21 (© Roger Wilmshurst); Photoshot pp. 12 (© NHPA/Stephen Dalton), 19 (Bruce Coleman/ Christer Fredriksson)); © Roger Scruton pp. 9, 14, 15, 17, 23, 29 top right); Shutterstock pp. 4 (© Kanwarjit Singh Boparai), 10 (© Andrew Bazylchik), 11 (© Marek Pawluczuk), 18 (© kml), 22 (© Samantha Grandy), 25 (© Kati Molin), 28 right (© Andrew Bazylchik), 29 bottom (© kml); Visuals Unlimited pp. 7 (© Nigel Cattlin), 8 (© Nigel Cattlin), 16 (© Nigel Cattlin), 28 left (© Nigel Cattlin).

Cover photograph reproduced with permission of Visuals Unlimited, Inc. (© Gap Photo/Graham Strong).

We would like to thank Michael Bright for his invaluable help in the preparation of this book.

Every effort has been made to contact copyright holders of material reproduced in this book. Any omissions will be rectified in subsequent printings if notice is given to the publisher.

DUDLEY PUBLIC LIBRARIES

L

700144   SCH

          J634

Contents

Some words are shown in bold, **like this**. You can find out what they mean by looking in the glossary.

What is an apple?

These crab apples are very **sour**. People cook them with sugar to make jelly.

An apple is a kind of fruit that grows on a tree. There are thousands of different kinds of apple trees. Most apples are good to eat.

Late winter

Early spring

1 week later

Apple trees often grow in groups called **orchards**.

The apples in this book are called red delicious. They taste sweet and juicy. Every year each tree produces a new crop of apples.

Late winter

These apple trees are about 10 years old.

Apple trees do not have any leaves in winter. They rest during the cold months.

Late winter

Early spring

1 week later

twig

bud

Each twig is covered with tight **buds**.

Apple trees have many branches. The smallest branches are called **twigs**.

Early spring

Buds begin to open as the days get warmer.

Tiny leaves are inside the **buds** on apple trees. They push through the buds and grow bigger.

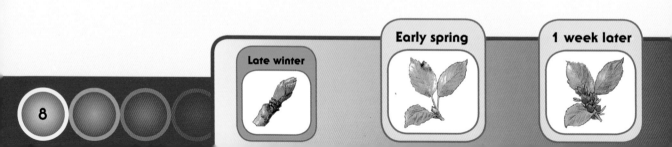

Late winter

Early spring

1 week later

Soon the whole tree is covered with leaves.

Leaves use water from the soil, sunlight, and air to make food for the tree. Pink buds grow among the leaves.

Spring

Flowers on fruit trees are called blossom.

One by one the pink **buds** open out into small pinkish-white flowers. Each flower has five petals with yellow **stamens** in the centre.

Late winter

Early spring

1 week later

Soon all the trees are covered with blossom.

Apple **blossom** has a sweet juice that honeybees like. It is called **nectar**.

Spring

4 weeks later

Summer

A few days later

Honeybees fly from flower to flower.

The **stamens** of apple **blossom** are covered in a yellow dust called **pollen**. Honeybees collect pollen as well as **nectar**.

Late winter	Early spring	1 week later

Honeybees store pollen on hairs on their back legs.

Some of the pollen from one flower rubs off onto the centre of the next flower. This pollen helps to make tiny apple seeds.

Spring

4 weeks later

Summer

4 weeks later

Four weeks later, the flower has done its job. Its petals dry up and die. Then they fall off.

A tiny apple is left after the petals of the apple **blossom** fall off.

Late winter

Early spring

1 week later

You can see what is left of the flower petals at one end of the little apples.

The apples begin to swell and grow.
The skin becomes waxy and shiny.

4 weeks later

Late spring

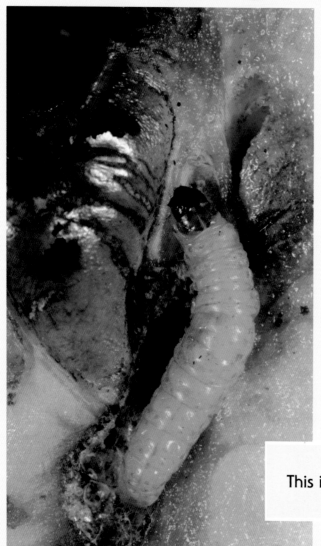

Many caterpillars and other insects like to eat the leaves and fruit of apple trees.

This is the caterpillar of a codling moth.

Late winter

Early spring

1 week later

A caterpillar has eaten a hole in this apple.

Many farmers spray their trees. This kills the insects that may damage the fruit.

Spring

4 weeks later

Summer

Summer

These big red apples are now sweet and **ripe**.

All summer the apples grow bigger. They get sweeter.

Late winter

Early spring

1 week later

This whole tree is covered with juicy red apples.

Soon all the apples are ready to be picked.

Early autumn

If apples are kept cool after they are picked, they will last all winter.

The apples are picked by hand. They are stored carefully in big boxes.

Late winter

Early spring

1 week later

Fallen apples make a nice meal for birds in the autumn.

Some of the apples fall to the ground before they are picked. Wasps and birds feed on them. Other fallen apples slowly rot.

Spring

4 weeks later

Summer

Late autumn

The red and yellow leaves will fall to the ground.

The apple trees are getting ready for winter. The leaves turn red and yellow.

Late winter

Early spring

1 week later

The apple trees lose all of their leaves. **Buds** form on the **twigs**. They will stay like this the whole winter.

The buds will open up into new leaves in the spring.

Winter

Farmers cut off some of the branches of their apple trees every winter. This helps to make the trees stronger.

Farmers use special tools to cut the branches.

Late winter

Early spring

1 week later

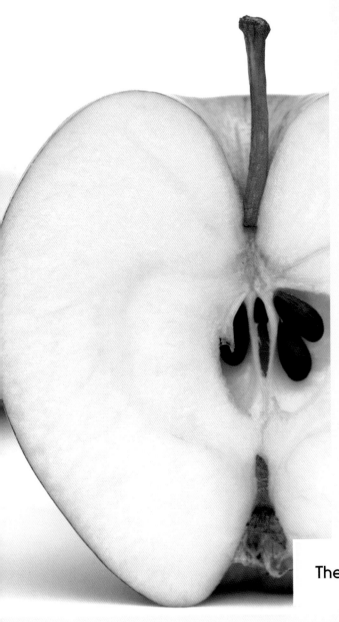

The brown pips inside each apple are seeds. If they are planted, they might grow into new apple trees in the spring.

The centre of an apple is called its core.

An apple orchard

Some apples will be sold to shops and markets. The rest will be made into pies or juice.

Thousands of apples grow in **orchards** each year.

Late winter

Early spring

1 week later

Apple trees start to make fruit at 3 to 5 years. Most farmers usually replace their trees before they are 20 years old.

These apple trees are only a few weeks old.

Life cycle

Late winter

Early spring

Spring

Early summer

Late summer

Fact file

- People have been eating apples for over 2 million years.

- Apple trees only produce good fruit in places that have a cold winter.

- We can eat apples all year round, because some countries have their autumn when we have our spring.

- One apple tree may produce about 200 apples each year.

- In a garden, some apple trees may live for up to 100 years.

Glossary

blossom flowers of a fruit tree

bud swelling on a stem or twig that will grow into leaves or a flower

nectar sweet juice that is in a flower

orchard field or garden where fruit trees are grown

pollen yellow dust that is in a flower

ripe fully grown and ready to eat

sour has a sharp taste

stamens yellow parts in the middle of a flower

twig thin branch

More books to read

From Seed to Apple (How Living Things Grow), Anita Ganeri (Heinemann Library, 2006)

The Life of an Apple, Clare Hibbert (Raintree, 2004)

Seeds (Plants), Patricia Whitehouse (Heinemann Library, 2009)

Index